THE FINANCIAL STORY OF JAMIE DIMON

His Strategic Leadership and Business Vision at JPMorgan Chase

FRANCIS A. FREDERICK

1

TABLE OF CONTENT

CHAPTER 1: BEGINNINGS OF A BUSINESS ICON

Jamie Dimon's journey to becoming one of the most influential figures in global finance began long before his tenure at JPMorgan Chase. His early life, characterized by a blend of academic rigor, family influences, and mentorship, laid a solid foundation for the business acumen he is known for today. Born on March 13, 1956, in New York City, Jamie Dimon was raised in a family that valued education and hard work.

His father, Theodore Dimon, was a stockbroker at Shearson, a firm that would later become part of the conglomerate Citigroup. This early exposure to the financial world had a profound impact on young Jamie. His grandfather, a Greek immigrant, had also worked in the financial industry, which made finance a family affair for the Dimons. Growing up in such an environment, Jamie naturally developed an interest in business and finance.

Jamie's upbringing was not just about business, though. His parents emphasized the importance of education and integrity. He attended the Browning School, an elite private school in Manhattan, where he was known for his academic prowess and leadership qualities. This early emphasis on excellence and ethical behavior would become a hallmark of his later career. After high school, Dimon enrolled at Tufts University, where he majored in psychology and economics.

It was here that he began to hone his analytical skills, blending an understanding of human behavior with economic theory—a combination that would prove invaluable in his career. He graduated summa cum laude in 1978, reflecting his dedication and intellect. Dimon's academic journey didn't end there. He went on to attend Harvard Business School, where he earned his MBA in 1982. His time at Harvard was transformative. Not only did he excel academically, but he also made connections that would shape his professional life. It was here that he first met his future mentor, Sanford "Sandy" Weill, who would play a pivotal role in Dimon's career.

During his summer breaks, Dimon worked at Goldman Sachs, gaining practical experience that complemented his academic training. His time at Harvard and Goldman Sachs solidified his interest in finance and prepared him for the challenges ahead. After graduating from Harvard, Dimon had offers from several prestigious firms, but he chose to work at American Express, where Sandy Weill was serving as President.

This decision was influenced by his admiration for Weill's strategic thinking and leadership style. At American Express, Dimon started as an assistant to Weill, a role that provided him with a front-row seat to high-level decision-making. Working closely with Weill, Dimon learned invaluable lessons about mergers, acquisitions, and corporate restructuring. Weill's hands-on approach to leadership and his ability to navigate complex business challenges left a lasting impression on Dimon. He learned the importance of understanding the details of every deal and the value of building strong relationships within the industry.

One of the key lessons Dimon took from his time at American Express was the importance of adaptability. The financial industry was undergoing significant changes, and companies had to be agile to survive and thrive. Dimon saw firsthand how Weill steered American Express through turbulent times, using strategic acquisitions to strengthen the company's position. This experience would later influence Dimon's own approach to leadership and strategy.

Dimon's relationship with Sandy Weill was more than just professional; it was a mentorship that deeply influenced his career trajectory. Weill, known for his aggressive yet calculated business strategies, took Dimon under his wing, teaching him the intricacies of the financial world. They formed a formidable team, with Dimon often described as Weill's "right-hand man." Their collaboration extended beyond American Express. When Weill left to head Commercial Credit, a small consumer finance company, Dimon followed.

Together, they transformed Commercial Credit into a financial powerhouse through a series of mergers and acquisitions, culminating in the creation of Citigroup. Dimon's role in this transformation was crucial, as he was responsible for integrating the various companies they acquired and ensuring the smooth operation of the newly formed conglomerate. This period was marked by intense challenges, including regulatory scrutiny and internal conflicts. However, it was also a time of immense learning for Dimon.

He developed a keen understanding of corporate strategy and the importance of resilience in the face of adversity. Jamie Dimon's early life and career were characterized by a unique combination of academic excellence, strategic mentorship, and practical experience. From his formative years in a financially savvy family to his rigorous academic training at Tufts and Harvard, Dimon was well-prepared for the challenges of the business world. His early career at American Express and his close relationship with Sandy Weill provided him with a strong foundation in leadership and strategy.

These experiences not only shaped his approach to business but also prepared him for the pivotal roles he would later assume at Bank One and JPMorgan Chase. As we delve further into his career, we will see how these early lessons and experiences propelled him to the top of the financial industry, allowing him to navigate some of the most challenging periods in modern financial history.

CHAPTER 2: CLIMBING THE CORPORATE LADDER

Jamie Dimon's career is a story of tenacity, bold decisions, and a relentless pursuit of excellence. After making a name for himself at American Express, Dimon faced one of the most transformative periods of his career at Commercial Credit and, eventually, Citigroup. This chapter delves into his journey through these challenging times, his decisions that shaped the future of global finance, and the invaluable lessons he learned along the way.

In 1985, Jamie Dimon followed his mentor, Sandy Weill, to Commercial Credit, a relatively small consumer finance company at the time. This move was a significant risk. Dimon had a stable position at American Express, but he chose to leave the comfort of a well-established firm to join Weill in rebuilding a lesser-known company.

This decision reflected Dimon's belief in Weill's vision and his willingness to take calculated risks—a trait that would define his career. At Commercial Credit, Dimon took on the role of Chief Financial Officer. He was tasked with stabilizing the company's finances and preparing it for growth. His work ethic and keen eye for detail played a crucial role in transforming Commercial Credit into a profitable entity. Dimon and Weill embarked on an ambitious plan to acquire struggling companies, using them as building blocks to create a financial powerhouse.

This aggressive acquisition strategy set the stage for the formation of a banking giant. The acquisition spree began with the purchase of Primerica, a financial services company, in 1988. This move marked the beginning of a series of mergers and acquisitions that would culminate in the formation of Citigroup, one of the largest financial institutions in the world. Dimon's role in these deals was critical. He was responsible for conducting thorough due diligence, negotiating terms, and integrating the acquired companies into a cohesive entity. His meticulous approach ensured that these acquisitions were not just financially sound but also strategically aligned with their long-term vision. The merger with Travelers Group in 1998 was a defining moment. It combined Commercial Credit, Primerica, Smith Barney, and other companies under one umbrella, creating a financial services behemoth. The formation of Citigroup represented a new era in the financial industry, offering a one-stop shop for a wide range of financial products and services.

Dimon's strategic thinking and operational expertise were instrumental in navigating the complexities of such a massive merger. He understood that simply merging companies was not enough; it was essential to create a unified culture and streamline operations to realize the full potential of the new conglomerate. This task was daunting, but Dimon's leadership was up to the challenge. The formation of Citigroup was not without its challenges. Integrating diverse companies with different cultures, systems, and processes required immense effort and coordination.

There were also significant regulatory hurdles, as the merger tested the boundaries of existing laws that separated commercial banking, investment banking, and insurance. Internally, conflicts began to emerge between Dimon and Weill. While they had worked closely for years, their relationship became strained as they navigated the complexities of managing the newly formed Citigroup. Dimon's meticulous attention to detail and his insistence on transparency sometimes clashed with Weill's more aggressive and opportunistic approach.

The tension reached a breaking point in 1999 when Dimon left Citigroup. His departure was sudden and surprising, given his crucial role in building the company. Many speculated that personal and professional differences between Dimon and Weill were the cause. Despite this setback, Dimon's reputation as a brilliant strategist and leader remained intact. Dimon's early career decisions and management style played a significant role in shaping his future success.

His decision to follow Weill to Commercial Credit demonstrated his willingness to take risks and his commitment to long-term vision over short-term stability. This decision not only propelled his career but also gave him the opportunity to develop a diverse set of skills in finance, mergers, and management. His management style, characterized by meticulous planning and a hands-on approach, was evident in every acquisition and merger he handled.

Dimon believed in understanding every aspect of the business, from financials to personnel, and this attention to detail set him apart from many of his peers. He was not afraid to make tough decisions, whether it was restructuring a struggling company or standing his ground against powerful figures like Weill. Dimon's departure from Citigroup was a pivotal moment. It was a humbling experience, but it also freed him from the shadow of his mentor and allowed him to forge his own path. His resilience and ability to learn from setbacks would serve him well in his future endeavors.

Dimon's experiences at Commercial Credit and Citigroup taught him several valuable lessons. He learned the importance of adaptability, as the financial industry was undergoing rapid changes during this period. He also realized the value of building a strong organizational culture, one that could withstand the pressures of rapid growth and complex integrations.

One of the most critical insights he gained was the importance of clear communication and alignment within leadership teams. The conflicts he faced at Citigroup highlighted the dangers of misaligned visions and the need for leaders to be on the same page. This lesson would later influence his leadership style at JPMorgan Chase, where he prioritized transparency and collaboration among his executive team. Jamie Dimon's journey through Commercial Credit and Citigroup was a transformative period that shaped his approach to leadership and strategy.

His willingness to take risks, his meticulous management style, and his ability to learn from conflicts and setbacks prepared him for the challenges that lay ahead. As we continue exploring his career, it becomes clear that these early experiences were instrumental in his rise to the top of the financial world.

CHAPTER 3: TURNING SETBACKS INTO COMEBACKS

Jamie Dimon's departure from Citigroup in 1998 was more than just a career setback; it was a personal and professional upheaval. After years of working closely with his mentor, Sandy Weill, to build one of the largest financial institutions in the world, Dimon suddenly found himself without a job, and more importantly, without direction.

This chapter explores how Dimon transformed this challenging period into a powerful comeback, leveraging his resilience and strategic insight to reestablish himself as a formidable leader in the financial world. Leaving Citigroup was a pivotal moment in Dimon's career. The circumstances surrounding his departure were complex and, at times, contentious. Despite being a key player in the formation of Citigroup, Dimon's relationship with Weill had deteriorated over time due to differing visions and management styles. Their disagreements culminated in Dimon's abrupt exit, leaving him sidelined in an industry he had helped shape. For many, this kind of professional blow would have been a career-ender. But for Dimon, it was a moment of reflection and recalibration. He took a year off, spending time with his family and considering his next steps. It was during this period that he gained a deeper understanding of his strengths and clarified what he wanted from his career.

Rather than jumping into another role immediately, Dimon waited for the right opportunity—one that would allow him to rebuild his legacy on his own terms. Dimon's approach to overcoming adversity was grounded in self-awareness and patience. Instead of rushing into another high-profile position, he took the time to carefully evaluate his options. He focused on identifying opportunities where he could make a meaningful impact, rather than seeking roles that offered immediate prestige or financial gain.

Networking and maintaining relationships were also critical components of his strategy. Despite his departure from Citigroup, Dimon remained well-connected in the industry. He leveraged these connections to stay informed about potential opportunities and to keep his name relevant in the financial community. This network would eventually lead him to his next major role at Bank One. Another key element of Dimon's strategy was his commitment to continuous learning.

During his time away from the corporate world, he stayed updated on industry trends and emerging challenges. This proactive approach ensured that when the right opportunity came along, he was prepared to step in and lead effectively. In 2000, Dimon joined Bank One, a struggling regional bank based in Chicago. The bank was grappling with declining profits, a demoralized workforce, and a lack of clear direction. For Dimon, this was the opportunity he had been waiting for—a chance to prove his capabilities and turn a troubled institution into a thriving business.

Dimon's first priority at Bank One was to stabilize the organization. He started by cutting costs and improving operational efficiency. This involved difficult decisions, including closing unprofitable branches and reducing the workforce. While these measures were initially unpopular, they were necessary to stop the financial bleeding and set the bank on a path to recovery. Next, Dimon focused on rebuilding the bank's culture. He believed that a strong, cohesive culture was essential for long-term success.

To achieve this, he spent significant time communicating with employees at all levels, listening to their concerns, and sharing his vision for the bank's future. This open and transparent approach helped rebuild trust and morale within the organization. Dimon also emphasized the importance of customer service and innovation. He invested in technology to improve the bank's online and mobile banking platforms, making it easier for customers to manage their finances. This focus on customer experience helped Bank One differentiate itself in a competitive market and attract new clients.

By 2004, Dimon had successfully turned around Bank One, making it one of the most profitable regional banks in the United States. His leadership not only restored the bank's financial health but also positioned it as an attractive merger partner. This led to the historic merger with JPMorgan Chase, a move that would once again elevate Dimon to the top ranks of the financial industry. Dimon's ability to turn setbacks into comebacks can be attributed to his resilience and strategic vision.

He demonstrated an extraordinary capacity to remain focused and composed under pressure, using setbacks as opportunities for growth and reinvention. His experience at Bank One was a testament to his belief that with the right strategy and leadership, any challenge can be overcome. Dimon's strategic vision was evident in his approach to the merger with JPMorgan Chase. He understood that the financial industry was becoming increasingly consolidated and that scale would be a critical factor for success. By merging Bank One with JPMorgan Chase, he created one of the largest and most diversified financial institutions in the world.

This move not only secured his place at the helm of a major global bank but also positioned JPMorgan Chase for sustained growth and stability. Jamie Dimon's journey from his departure at Citigroup to his triumph at Bank One is a powerful example of resilience and strategic foresight. His ability to navigate adversity, coupled with his unwavering commitment to excellence, set the stage for his next big move—leading JPMorgan Chase through some of the most challenging periods in modern financial history. As we move forward in this narrative, it becomes clear that Dimon's career is not just about success but also about the courage to face failure and the wisdom to turn it into a foundation for future victories.

CHAPTER 4: THE JPMORGAN CHASE ERA BEGINS

Jamie Dimon's entry into JPMorgan Chase marked a turning point not just for the bank, but for the entire financial industry. The merger between Bank One and JPMorgan Chase in 2004 was more than just a business transaction; it was the beginning of a new era. Dimon's strategic vision, combined with his hands-on management style, transformed the newly merged entity into one of the most formidable banking institutions in the world.

This chapter delves into the early challenges of the merger, Dimon's rise to CEO, and the strategic initiatives that defined his leadership during those initial years. The merger of Bank One and JPMorgan Chase was a bold move that created the second-largest bank in the United States at the time. When the deal was announced in

January 2004, it was valued at approximately $58 billion.

For Jamie Dimon, who had successfully turned around Bank One, this merger was an opportunity to showcase his leadership on a much larger stage. Dimon's appointment as President and Chief Operating Officer of JPMorgan Chase positioned him as the heir apparent to then-CEO William Harrison. This transition period allowed Dimon to get a handle on the complexities of the combined entity before taking over as CEO in 2005. The merger was not just about expanding size; it was about integrating two very different cultures and operational systems into a cohesive whole.

The integration of Bank One and JPMorgan Chase was a monumental task. The two banks had different operating systems, corporate cultures, and customer bases. Dimon knew that to make the merger successful, he would need to address these differences head-on. One of the first steps he took was to streamline the bank's technology systems. This involved significant investments in IT infrastructure to ensure that both banks operated on the same platforms.

It was a costly and time-consuming process, but it was necessary to create a unified organization. Cultural integration was another major challenge. Bank One was known for its no-nonsense, cost-conscious culture, while JPMorgan Chase had a more traditional, hierarchical structure. Dimon set out to create a new culture that combined the best elements of both organizations. He encouraged open communication, broke down silos, and promoted a sense of shared purpose.

His leadership style was direct and transparent, which helped to build trust among employees during this period of significant change. Additionally, Dimon faced external challenges, including regulatory scrutiny and market skepticism about whether the merger would deliver the promised benefits. He responded by maintaining a focus on execution, demonstrating through results that the combined entity was stronger and more efficient than its predecessors. As CEO, one of Dimon's first major tasks was to rebuild and restructure JPMorgan Chase.

The bank was still recovering from the aftermath of the 2001 recession, and its performance was lagging behind its competitors. Dimon took a proactive approach, focusing on cost-cutting measures and operational efficiency. He streamlined business units, reduced redundant roles, and renegotiated contracts with suppliers to save costs. Dimon also focused on strengthening the bank's balance sheet. He improved the risk management framework and increased the bank's capital reserves.

This conservative approach to risk was a departure from the more aggressive strategies employed by some of JPMorgan Chase's competitors, but it would prove to be a crucial factor in the bank's resilience during the financial crisis of 2008. Another critical aspect of Dimon's restructuring efforts was the focus on customer service and innovation. He recognized that to compete effectively, the bank needed to offer more than just traditional financial services. Under his leadership,

JPMorgan Chase invested heavily in digital banking and technology, enhancing its online and mobile banking platforms to improve customer experience. These initiatives not only helped to attract new customers but also solidified the bank's reputation as a leader in financial technology. Dimon's early strategic initiatives at JPMorgan Chase set the stage for the bank's future success. One of his first major moves was the acquisition of Bank of New York's retail banking business. This deal, completed in 2006, expanded JPMorgan Chase's footprint in the highly competitive New York market and added over 300 branches to its network.

Another key initiative was the acquisition of Bear Stearns in 2008. At the height of the financial crisis, Bear Stearns was on the verge of collapse, and its failure threatened to destabilize the entire financial system. Dimon's decision to acquire Bear Stearns for a fraction of its pre-crisis value was both bold and controversial. It positioned JPMorgan Chase as a stabilizing force in the market and solidified Dimon's reputation as a decisive leader capable of making tough decisions under pressure.

Dimon also focused on expanding JPMorgan Chase's global presence. He recognized the importance of international markets for future growth and made strategic investments in regions such as Asia and Latin America. This global expansion strategy not only diversified the bank's revenue streams but also reduced its dependence on the U.S. market. Throughout these early years, Dimon's leadership was characterized by a relentless focus on execution and results.

He was not afraid to make unpopular decisions if he believed they were in the best long-term interest of the bank. His ability to balance short-term challenges with long-term strategic vision enabled JPMorgan Chase to navigate through one of the most turbulent periods in financial history and emerge stronger than ever. Jamie Dimon's early years at JPMorgan Chase were marked by significant challenges and bold strategic moves. His leadership during this period laid the groundwork for the bank's transformation into a global financial powerhouse.

Dimon's ability to integrate diverse organizations, rebuild a struggling entity, and execute strategic initiatives with precision are testaments to his exceptional leadership and vision. As we move forward in this narrative, it becomes clear that these early years were just the beginning of Dimon's impact on the world of finance.

CHAPTER 5: NAVIGATING THE 2008 FINANCIAL CRISIS

Jamie Dimon's leadership during the 2008 financial crisis is often cited as a defining moment in his career and a crucial period for JPMorgan Chase. While many financial institutions struggled to survive, Dimon's strategic foresight and decisive actions helped position JPMorgan Chase not only to withstand the turmoil but to emerge stronger.

This chapter delves into the pivotal role he played, the strategies he employed, and the lessons learned from navigating one of the most challenging periods in modern financial history. When the financial crisis hit in 2008, it was a storm that few saw coming in its full magnitude. Banks were collapsing, markets were in freefall, and the global economy teetered on the brink of a complete meltdown. Jamie Dimon, who had already made a name for himself as a steady and pragmatic leader, found himself at the forefront of navigating these turbulent waters. Dimon's approach was marked by caution and preparation long before the crisis fully erupted. He had been voicing concerns about the housing market and the excessive risk-taking practices of many financial institutions. His skepticism led JPMorgan Chase to limit its exposure to risky mortgage-backed securities, which were at the heart of the financial meltdown. This conservative stance meant that when the crisis did hit, JPMorgan Chase was in a relatively stronger position compared to many of its peers.

Dimon's strategy during the crisis can be summarized in three key principles: liquidity, risk management, and opportunistic acquisitions.

1. Maintaining Liquidity: One of Dimon's first priorities was to ensure that JPMorgan Chase had ample liquidity to weather the storm. He understood that during times of financial panic, cash is king. By maintaining a strong cash position, the bank was able to navigate through market disruptions without having to resort to desperate measures, such as fire sales of assets or seeking government bailouts.

2. Strengthening Risk Management: Dimon placed a strong emphasis on risk management. He worked closely with the bank's risk officers to identify and mitigate potential threats. This involved not only limiting exposure to toxic assets but also ensuring that the bank's balance sheet remained strong and transparent. This rigorous approach to risk management helped the bank avoid the worst of the crisis and maintain the confidence of its investors and customers.

3. Opportunistic Acquisitions: Perhaps the most visible aspect of Dimon's strategy was his willingness to make bold acquisitions during the height of the crisis. When Bear Stearns, a major investment bank, found itself on the verge of collapse in March 2008, Dimon saw an opportunity. With the support of the Federal Reserve, JPMorgan Chase acquired Bear Stearns for a fraction of its previous value. This move was risky, as it involved taking on significant liabilities, but it also allowed

JPMorgan Chase to gain valuable assets and strengthen its position in the investment banking sector.

Later that same year, Dimon made another bold move by acquiring the banking operations of Washington Mutual (WaMu) after it was seized by regulators. This acquisition, which cost JPMorgan Chase $1.9 billion, expanded the bank's retail footprint significantly, adding millions of new customers and thousands of branches, particularly in key markets like California and Florida.

The acquisitions of Bear Stearns and Washington Mutual were transformative for JPMorgan Chase. While they came with significant risks and challenges, they also offered substantial rewards. The Bear Stearns acquisition gave JPMorgan Chase a stronger presence in investment banking, while the Washington Mutual deal expanded its retail banking network. However, these acquisitions were not without their difficulties. Integrating the two companies required significant resources and effort.

There were cultural differences, technology integration issues, and a need to manage the reputational risks associated with acquiring distressed assets. Despite these challenges, Dimon's steady leadership and clear vision enabled JPMorgan Chase to successfully absorb these entities and leverage them to enhance the bank's overall strength and competitiveness.

Lessons Learned and Long-Term Effects

Dimon's handling of the financial crisis left a lasting impact on JPMorgan Chase and the broader financial industry. Several key lessons emerged from this period:

1. The Importance of Preparation: Dimon's emphasis on maintaining a strong balance sheet and robust risk management practices was instrumental in helping JPMorgan Chase navigate the crisis. This experience reinforced the importance of being prepared for worst-case scenarios and maintaining a conservative approach to risk.

2. Opportunism in Crisis: The acquisitions of Bear Stearns and Washington Mutual demonstrated that crises often present opportunities for those who are prepared and willing to act decisively. While these acquisitions involved significant risks, they ultimately strengthened JPMorgan Chase and positioned it as a leader in the industry.

3. The Value of Strong Leadership: Dimon's leadership during the crisis showcased his ability to make tough decisions under pressure. His clear communication, transparency, and willingness to take bold actions helped maintain confidence in JPMorgan Chase during a time of widespread uncertainty.

4. Long-Term Strategic Vision: The strategic moves made during the crisis set the stage for JPMorgan Chase's long-term growth. The bank emerged from the crisis larger and more diversified, with a stronger competitive position in both retail and investment banking.

In the aftermath of the crisis, Dimon's reputation as one of the most effective and respected leaders in finance was solidified. His ability to steer JPMorgan Chase through such a turbulent period without requiring a government bailout, and his skill in turning adversity into opportunity, earned him widespread admiration.

As we move forward in this narrative, it becomes clear that Dimon's experience during the 2008 financial crisis was not just a test of his leadership but also a testament to his strategic foresight and resilience. The lessons learned during this period continue to influence his approach to managing risk and navigating challenges in an ever-evolving financial landscape.

CHAPTER 6: INNOVATIONS AND STRATEGIC EXPANSION

Jamie Dimon has always been a visionary leader, constantly looking ahead to see where the financial industry is going and how JPMorgan Chase can not only keep up but lead the way. Under his leadership, the bank has undergone a remarkable transformation, embracing technology and innovation to expand its global footprint and offer cutting-edge financial solutions.

This chapter explores Dimon's strategic initiatives, focusing on digital transformation, global expansion, and innovative financial strategies that have cemented JPMorgan Chase's position as a global financial powerhouse. When Jamie Dimon took over as CEO, he envisioned JPMorgan Chase not just as a dominant player in the U.S. but as a leading global financial institution. He understood that to achieve this, the bank needed to be more than just big; it had to be agile, innovative, and customer-focused.

His vision was to create a bank that could seamlessly operate across borders, providing clients with the best financial products and services, whether they were individuals, corporations, or governments. Dimon's strategy involved expanding the bank's global presence through acquisitions, partnerships, and organic growth. He focused on strengthening JPMorgan Chase's presence in key international markets, such as Europe, Asia, and Latin America.

This global push was not just about increasing the bank's size; it was about creating a truly integrated financial institution that could serve clients' needs wherever they were in the world. One of the most significant aspects of Dimon's leadership has been his commitment to digital transformation. He recognized early on that technology would be a key driver of future growth in the financial industry. Under his guidance, JPMorgan Chase has invested billions in technology, not just to improve its internal operations but also to enhance the customer experience.

Dimon's focus on digital transformation is evident in several key initiatives. One of the most notable is the development of the bank's mobile and online banking platforms. JPMorgan Chase was one of the first major banks to invest heavily in digital banking, creating a seamless and user-friendly experience for its customers. This move not only attracted tech-savvy customers but also set a new standard for the industry.

In addition to retail banking, Dimon has pushed for technological advancements in other areas of the bank's operations, including trading, risk management, and compliance. The adoption of artificial intelligence and machine learning has allowed JPMorgan Chase to better analyze data, predict market trends, and manage risk more effectively. For instance, the bank's use of AI in fraud detection has significantly reduced the incidence of fraudulent transactions, protecting both the bank and its customers. Dimon's strategy for global expansion has been multifaceted. He has pursued a mix of acquisitions, partnerships, and organic growth to build the bank's presence in key international markets.

One of the most successful examples of this strategy is JPMorgan Chase's expansion in China. Recognizing the importance of the Chinese market, Dimon worked to secure regulatory approvals that allowed the bank to increase its stake in its Chinese securities joint venture, making JPMorgan Chase the first foreign bank to fully own its securities business in China. This move positioned the bank to capitalize on the growing demand for financial services in one of the world's largest and fastest-growing economies.

In Europe, Dimon has focused on expanding the bank's operations in key financial hubs such as London and Frankfurt. Despite the uncertainties surrounding Brexit, Dimon saw an opportunity to strengthen the bank's presence on the continent. He spearheaded the expansion of JPMorgan Chase's office in Paris, positioning it as a major hub for the bank's European operations. Risk management has always been a cornerstone of Dimon's leadership philosophy. He understands that while innovation and expansion are essential, they must be balanced with prudent risk management practices.

This approach has helped JPMorgan Chase navigate numerous financial storms, including the 2008 crisis, with minimal damage compared to its peers. Dimon's focus on risk management is reflected in the bank's investment in technology and analytics to better understand and mitigate risks. For example, the bank uses advanced algorithms to monitor and manage market and credit risks in real-time, enabling it to make informed decisions quickly.

In addition to traditional banking services, Dimon has pushed for innovation in financial solutions. One of the most significant initiatives in this regard is the development of JPM Coin, a digital currency designed to facilitate instantaneous payments between institutional clients. This move into digital currencies is a testament to Dimon's forward-thinking approach and willingness to explore new financial technologies. Dimon's tenure at JPMorgan Chase is marked by several successful ventures and strategic investments that have significantly enhanced the bank's capabilities and market position.

One such example is the acquisition of WePay in 2017, a fintech company specializing in integrated payments for online platforms. This acquisition allowed JPMorgan Chase to expand its capabilities in the rapidly growing digital payments space, catering to the needs of small businesses and entrepreneurs. Another notable venture is the bank's investment in blockchain technology.

Recognizing the potential of blockchain to revolutionize the financial industry, Dimon has overseen the development of several blockchain-based solutions, including the Interbank Information Network (IIN), which uses blockchain to streamline cross-border payments and reduce transaction times. His vision for JPMorgan Chase has been transformative. His focus on digital transformation, global expansion, and innovative financial solutions has positioned the bank as a leader in the industry, capable of navigating the complexities of a rapidly changing financial landscape.

Dimon's strategic initiatives have not only strengthened the bank's market position but also set a new standard for what a global financial institution can achieve. As we continue exploring his leadership journey, it becomes clear that Dimon's commitment to innovation and growth is a driving force behind JPMorgan Chase's success.

CHAPTER 7: LEADERSHIP PHILOSOPHY AND MANAGEMENT STYLE

Jamie Dimon's leadership style has been a subject of much discussion and admiration within the business world. As the CEO of JPMorgan Chase, he has guided the bank through economic downturns, regulatory challenges, and significant industry shifts. His leadership philosophy is rooted in clear decision-making, effective communication, and a deep commitment to the development of his team and the organization's culture.

This chapter explores Dimon's approach to leadership, his decision-making style, and the principles that have shaped his management over the years. At the core of Jamie Dimon's leadership philosophy is the belief in leading by example. He emphasizes integrity, transparency, and accountability, holding himself to the same high standards he expects of his team. Dimon is known for his hands-on approach, often getting involved in the details of the business to understand the challenges his employees face and to make informed decisions. He believes in confronting problems head-on and making tough decisions when necessary. "The road to hell is paved with good intentions," he often says, stressing the importance of not just having the right ideas but also executing them effectively. This no-nonsense approach has earned him a reputation as a decisive and pragmatic leader who does not shy away from difficult conversations or decisions.

Dimon's leadership philosophy also includes a strong emphasis on long-term thinking. He often advises against chasing short-term gains at the expense of sustainable growth and stability. This perspective has guided his decisions during times of crisis, such as the 2008 financial meltdown, where his focus was not just on immediate survival but on positioning JPMorgan Chase for long-term success. Dimon's approach to decision-making is both data-driven and intuitive. He values comprehensive data and analysis, but he also trusts his instincts, honed over decades of experience in the financial industry. He encourages his team to bring up different perspectives and to challenge his views, fostering an environment where diverse opinions are heard and valued. This approach not only improves decision quality but also empowers employees to speak up and contribute. Employee relations are a significant part of Dimon's management style. He believes in being approachable and accessible to his team, often walking the floors of JPMorgan Chase's offices to talk to employees at all levels.

He listens to their concerns and ideas, understanding that those on the front lines often have the best insights into what's working and what's not. This open-door policy has helped him build a strong rapport with his workforce and has contributed to a corporate culture that values collaboration and transparency. Corporate culture is something Dimon takes very seriously. He believes that the culture of an organization is what determines its success or failure over the long term.

At JPMorgan Chase, he has worked hard to create a culture that emphasizes ethical behavior, customer focus, and continuous improvement. He often says that it's not just about what you achieve but how you achieve it. This focus on ethics and integrity has helped the bank maintain its reputation, even during challenging times. Several key principles have guided Jamie Dimon's management style throughout his career. First and foremost is his commitment to integrity and ethical leadership.

He believes that trust is the foundation of any successful business and that leaders must act with honesty and transparency at all times. This principle has been particularly important in the banking industry, where trust is paramount. Another guiding principle is the importance of resilience and adaptability. Dimon often talks about the need to be prepared for unexpected challenges and to be able to pivot when circumstances change. This mindset has been crucial in navigating the many crises he has faced as a leader, from financial downturns to regulatory changes.

Dimon also places a strong emphasis on accountability. He believes that leaders should be willing to take responsibility for their decisions and actions, both good and bad. This means owning up to mistakes and learning from them, as well as giving credit to others when things go well. This principle of accountability extends to everyone in the organization, creating a culture where people feel empowered to take risks but also understand the importance of delivering results.

Finally, Dimon is a big proponent of continuous learning and development. He encourages his team to keep learning and to stay curious about the world around them. He believes that the best leaders are those who are constantly evolving and who are open to new ideas and perspectives. This commitment to growth and learning has been a key factor in his success and has helped JPMorgan Chase remain at the forefront of the financial industry. Colleagues and industry experts often describe Jamie Dimon as a leader who combines toughness with empathy.

He is known for being direct and demanding but also for genuinely caring about his employees and their well-being. Many who have worked with him speak of his ability to inspire and motivate, even during difficult times. Employees appreciate Dimon's transparency and his willingness to share both the good and the bad news. His regular town hall meetings and candid memos to staff have helped build a sense of trust and openness within the organization.

He is not afraid to tackle tough issues head-on, whether it's addressing financial challenges or discussing broader social and economic issues. Industry experts often point to Dimon's ability to balance risk and opportunity as one of his greatest strengths. They admire his strategic vision and his skill in navigating complex and volatile environments. His leadership during the 2008 financial crisis is frequently cited as a textbook example of effective crisis management, and his ongoing efforts to innovate and expand JPMorgan Chase demonstrate his forward-thinking approach.

Jamie Dimon's leadership philosophy and management style are characterized by a strong commitment to integrity, a focus on long-term success, and a deep respect for the people who work for him. His ability to make tough decisions while maintaining a positive and inclusive corporate culture has made him one of the most respected leaders in the business world. As we continue to explore his career, it is clear that his leadership principles and management approach will have a lasting impact not just on JPMorgan Chase but on the broader financial industry.

CHAPTER 8: CHALLENGES IN THE MODERN FINANCIAL LANDSCAPE

Jamie Dimon, the CEO of JPMorgan Chase, has navigated the financial industry through various challenges and transformations over the years. Today, the modern financial landscape presents new complexities, such as regulatory changes, cybersecurity threats, the rise of cryptocurrencies, and economic instability. Dimon's views on these issues reflect his experience and his forward-looking approach to leadership.

This chapter explores his perspectives on these challenges, how he has positioned JPMorgan Chase to remain competitive, and his insights on inflation and economic stability in 2024. Regulatory changes are a constant challenge for financial institutions, and Dimon has been vocal about the need for balanced regulation that ensures market stability without stifling innovation.

He believes that while regulations are necessary to prevent the kind of risky behavior that led to the 2008 financial crisis, they should be implemented thoughtfully to avoid unintended consequences that could harm the economy. One of Dimon's key concerns is the complexity and cost of compliance. For large banks like JPMorgan Chase, the resources required to comply with an ever-expanding set of rules can be substantial. Dimon has argued that excessive regulation can reduce the competitiveness of U.S. financial institutions, particularly in the global market.

He advocates for regulations that are clear, consistent, and designed to promote stability without creating unnecessary burdens for businesses. In terms of market volatility, Dimon's stance is one of caution and preparedness. He has often highlighted the importance of maintaining a strong balance sheet and liquidity to weather financial storms. His approach to managing JPMorgan Chase has always been conservative when it comes to risk, ensuring that the bank is well-positioned to handle market fluctuations. He emphasizes that while volatility is a natural part of the financial markets, institutions must be resilient and agile to adapt to changing conditions. Dimon's views on cryptocurrency have evolved over the years. Initially, he was a vocal critic, famously calling Bitcoin a "fraud" in 2017. However, he has since acknowledged the potential of blockchain technology and digital currencies, albeit with caution.

Dimon distinguishes between cryptocurrencies like Bitcoin, which he remains skeptical about, and the underlying blockchain technology, which he sees as having significant potential for improving the efficiency and security of financial transactions. Under Dimon's leadership, JPMorgan Chase has taken steps to embrace blockchain technology. The bank developed its own digital currency, JPM Coin, to facilitate instant payments between institutional clients. This move reflects Dimon's recognition that blockchain can streamline financial processes and reduce costs.

Additionally, JPMorgan has launched Onyx, a business unit focused on building blockchain-based platforms and products, signaling a strategic shift towards exploring the benefits of this technology. Despite these advancements, Dimon remains cautious about the broader adoption of cryptocurrencies. He has expressed concerns about their use in illegal activities and the lack of regulatory oversight.

While he supports innovation, he believes that governments need to establish a regulatory framework for cryptocurrencies to ensure that they are used safely and responsibly. To maintain a competitive edge in the evolving financial industry, Dimon has focused on several key strategies: innovation, customer focus, and global expansion. He believes that continuous innovation is essential for staying ahead in a rapidly changing market. This is why JPMorgan Chase invests heavily in technology, not only to improve internal operations but also to enhance the customer experience.

Digital transformation has been a cornerstone of Dimon's strategy. The bank has developed advanced digital banking platforms that offer seamless, user-friendly experiences for its customers. These platforms are designed to meet the needs of a tech-savvy customer base that expects convenience and efficiency. By investing in digital solutions, JPMorgan Chase aims to attract and retain customers while setting a high standard for the industry.

Another key aspect of Dimon's strategy is global expansion. He has worked to strengthen the bank's presence in key international markets, recognizing that growth opportunities are not limited to the United States. By expanding its footprint in regions like Asia and Europe, JPMorgan Chase can diversify its revenue streams and reduce its dependence on any single market. Finally, Dimon's focus on risk management is a critical part of maintaining the bank's competitive edge. He understands that in an industry as volatile as finance, being able to manage and mitigate risk is essential.

This is why JPMorgan Chase has invested in advanced risk management systems and analytics to ensure that it can respond quickly to emerging threats and opportunities. In recent years, Dimon has been outspoken about the risks posed by rising inflation. He believes that the current economic environment is characterized by a combination of factors that could lead to sustained inflationary pressures. These include high government debt, expansive fiscal policies, and disruptions in global supply chains.

Dimon's concern is that the Federal Reserve and other central banks may struggle to contain inflation without triggering a recession. He has warned that the measures required to bring inflation under control, such as raising interest rates, could have a significant impact on economic growth and employment. Despite these challenges, he advocates for a proactive approach, arguing that it is better to address inflation early rather than allowing it to become entrenched.

To manage these risks, Dimon has ensured that JPMorgan Chase remains financially strong and flexible. The bank has increased its capital reserves and liquidity, positioning itself to weather potential economic downturns. This conservative approach to risk management reflects Dimon's belief that stability and resilience are the keys to navigating uncertain times. Jamie Dimon's leadership in the modern financial landscape is marked by his ability to balance innovation with caution.

Whether it's embracing new technologies like blockchain, expanding into global markets, or preparing for economic uncertainty, Dimon's approach is rooted in a deep understanding of the complexities of the financial world. His insights on regulatory challenges, market volatility, and economic stability continue to shape the strategic direction of JPMorgan Chase, ensuring that the bank remains a leader in the industry. As the financial landscape continues to evolve, Dimon's leadership will undoubtedly be a guiding force for the bank and a benchmark for others in the industry.

CHAPTER 9: THE ROAD AHEAD FOR JPMORGAN CHASE

Jamie Dimon has been at the helm of JPMorgan Chase for nearly two decades, guiding the bank through economic crises, regulatory changes, and significant transformations. As the financial landscape continues to evolve, the future of JPMorgan Chase under Dimon's leadership remains a topic of considerable interest.

This chapter explores the potential challenges and opportunities that lie ahead for the bank, Dimon's plans for succession, and his impact on the next generation of financial leaders. JPMorgan Chase has established itself as a global financial powerhouse, and much of its success can be attributed to Dimon's strategic vision and steady leadership. Looking ahead, Dimon's focus remains on maintaining the bank's strong financial position while continuing to innovate and adapt to the changing market dynamics.

He is known for his forward-thinking approach and his ability to anticipate industry trends, which has positioned JPMorgan Chase as a leader in digital transformation and global expansion. Dimon's current priorities include enhancing the bank's digital capabilities, expanding its presence in key international markets, and strengthening its position in emerging areas such as fintech and sustainable finance.

He has emphasized the importance of leveraging technology to improve customer experience and operational efficiency. This focus on innovation is expected to keep JPMorgan Chase at the forefront of the financial industry, even as new competitors emerge. Another key area of focus for Dimon is sustainable finance. As environmental, social, and governance (ESG) considerations become increasingly important to investors and regulators, JPMorgan Chase is working to integrate these principles into its business strategy. The bank has committed to financing and facilitating more than $2.5 trillion over ten years to address climate change and promote sustainable development.

This commitment reflects Dimon's belief that financial institutions have a critical role to play in addressing global challenges and supporting sustainable economic growth. The global financial market is constantly evolving, and JPMorgan Chase faces several challenges and opportunities as it navigates this complex environment. One of the most significant challenges is the increasing regulatory scrutiny on large financial institutions.

As governments and regulators around the world seek to prevent another financial crisis, they are imposing stricter rules on capital requirements, risk management, and compliance. Dimon has expressed concern that excessive regulation could stifle innovation and hinder the bank's ability to compete globally. Balancing regulatory compliance with the need for flexibility and growth will be a critical challenge for JPMorgan Chase in the years ahead. Another challenge is the rapid pace of technological change. The rise of fintech companies and digital banking platforms is disrupting traditional banking models, and JPMorgan Chase must continue to innovate to stay competitive. Dimon has recognized this threat and has made significant investments in technology, including artificial intelligence, blockchain, and cybersecurity. By staying at the cutting edge of technological innovation, the bank aims to enhance its services, reduce costs, and protect against emerging risks. Despite these challenges, there are also significant opportunities for growth. The expansion into emerging markets, particularly in Asia and Latin America, offers potential for increased revenues and market share.

Additionally, the ongoing shift towards digital finance presents opportunities for JPMorgan Chase to develop new products and services that meet the changing needs of its customers. One of the most discussed topics in recent years has been Dimon's succession plans. As a long-serving CEO, he has built a strong leadership team and a deep bench of talent at JPMorgan Chase. However, the question of who will succeed him remains a critical issue for the bank and its stakeholders.

Dimon has stated that he intends to stay on as CEO for as long as he is effective and enjoys the work, but he has also acknowledged the importance of preparing for the future. He has worked to develop a pipeline of potential successors, ensuring that the next generation of leaders is ready to take the reins when the time comes.

The bank's leadership team includes several experienced executives who are widely considered potential candidates for the top job, such as Daniel Pinto, co-president and chief operating officer, and Marianne Lake, the former chief financial officer. Dimon's approach to succession planning is characterized by his emphasis on continuity and stability. He wants to ensure that his successor is not only capable of managing the bank's day-to-day operations but also shares his long-term vision for its future. This careful planning reflects Dimon's commitment to leaving JPMorgan Chase in the best possible hands when he eventually steps down.

Jamie Dimon's leadership has had a profound impact on the financial industry, and his influence extends beyond JPMorgan Chase. His management style, characterized by transparency, accountability, and a focus on long-term growth, has set a standard for how modern financial institutions should be run. Dimon's willingness to take bold actions, such as acquiring Bear Stearns during the financial crisis, has shown that decisive leadership is essential in times of uncertainty.

For the next generation of financial professionals, Dimon's career offers valuable lessons in resilience, innovation, and ethical leadership. He has consistently emphasized the importance of integrity and responsibility in business, advocating for a culture that prioritizes doing what is right over what is easy. This message resonates with young professionals who are increasingly looking for purpose and values in their careers. Dimon's commitment to mentoring and developing talent within JPMorgan Chase has also left a lasting legacy.

He has created an environment where employees are encouraged to grow, take risks, and learn from their mistakes. This focus on personal and professional development has helped cultivate a strong, capable leadership team that will carry the bank forward in the years to come. The road ahead for JPMorgan Chase is filled with both challenges and opportunities. Under Jamie Dimon's leadership, the bank is well-positioned to navigate these complexities and continue its growth as a global financial leader. Dimon's strategic vision, commitment to innovation, and focus on developing the next generation of leaders will ensure that JPMorgan Chase remains at the forefront of the financial industry, ready to tackle whatever the future may hold.

CHAPTER 10: LEGACY OF A FINANCIAL TITAN

Jamie Dimon's career at the helm of JPMorgan Chase is nothing short of extraordinary. He has navigated the bank through some of the most challenging periods in financial history, all while solidifying its position as one of the most respected institutions in the world. As his tenure begins to wind down, it's an opportune moment to reflect on his contributions, the impact of his leadership on modern banking, and the lessons he leaves for aspiring business leaders and entrepreneurs.

Dimon's career trajectory is a testament to resilience, strategic foresight, and an unwavering commitment to excellence. From his early days at Commercial Credit and his tumultuous departure from Citigroup to his transformative leadership at JPMorgan Chase, Dimon has demonstrated an ability to turn challenges into opportunities. His role during the 2008 financial crisis is particularly noteworthy; while many institutions floundered, Dimon's steady hand and prudent risk management helped JPMorgan Chase not only survive but thrive. One of the most significant aspects of Dimon's legacy is his emphasis on long-term thinking. In an industry often criticized for short-termism, Dimon has consistently prioritized sustainable growth over quick profits. His focus on maintaining a strong balance sheet, investing in technology, and building a robust risk management framework has enabled JPMorgan Chase to navigate numerous market upheavals with resilience.

Dimon's influence extends beyond the walls of JPMorgan Chase. His candid commentary on economic and regulatory issues has made him a respected voice in the industry. He has often spoken out on topics such as financial reform, corporate governance, and the role of banks in society, providing a thoughtful perspective that balances the interests of shareholders, employees, and the broader community. Dimon's leadership has had a profound impact on how modern banks operate. One of his most significant contributions is his approach to risk management.

In the years leading up to the 2008 crisis, many banks took on excessive risk in pursuit of higher returns. Dimon, however, maintained a more conservative stance, ensuring that JPMorgan Chase had sufficient capital reserves and a diversified portfolio. This focus on risk management not only protected the bank during the crisis but also set a new standard for the industry. His commitment to digital transformation has also influenced modern banking practices.

Under his leadership, JPMorgan Chase has invested heavily in technology, enhancing its digital banking platforms and utilizing advanced data analytics to improve customer service and operational efficiency. This emphasis on technology has not only improved the bank's competitiveness but has also driven broader innovation in the financial services industry. Furthermore, Dimon's strategic acquisitions, such as the purchases of Bear Stearns and Washington Mutual, have demonstrated the importance of bold, well-timed decisions in achieving long-term success.

These acquisitions, made during a period of extreme market volatility, allowed JPMorgan Chase to expand its capabilities and market presence significantly. His willingness to take calculated risks has shown other business leaders the value of seizing opportunities, even in the face of uncertainty.

There are several key lessons that aspiring business leaders and entrepreneurs can learn from Jamie Dimon's career:

1. The Importance of Integrity and Accountability: Dimon has always emphasized the need for ethical leadership and taking responsibility for one's actions. He believes that trust is the foundation of any successful business relationship, whether with employees, customers, or shareholders. For future leaders, this means being transparent, owning up to mistakes, and consistently doing the right thing, even when it's difficult.

2. Focus on Long-Term Goals: Dimon's leadership demonstrates the value of thinking beyond immediate gains. He has often advised against focusing solely on quarterly results, advocating instead for strategies that drive sustainable growth and stability. This lesson is particularly relevant in today's fast-paced business environment, where the pressure for short-term results can lead to poor decision-making.

3. Resilience in the Face of Adversity: Throughout his career, Dimon has faced numerous setbacks, including his departure from Citigroup and the challenges of navigating the 2008 financial crisis. Each time, he has come back stronger, using adversity as an opportunity to learn and grow. For aspiring leaders, this highlights the importance of resilience and the ability to adapt to changing circumstances.

4. The Role of Technology and Innovation: Dimon's emphasis on digital transformation and innovation has been a key factor in JPMorgan Chase's success. He has shown that embracing new technologies and being open to change are crucial for staying competitive in any industry. Future leaders should take note of the need to continuously innovate and invest in technology to meet the evolving needs of customers and the market.

Jamie Dimon's contributions to the financial industry and society are significant and enduring. His leadership has not only shaped the trajectory of JPMorgan Chase but has also influenced broader discussions on the role of banks in the economy. He has advocated for responsible banking practices, improved regulatory frameworks, and greater financial inclusion, recognizing that banks have a responsibility to contribute positively to society. Beyond his professional achievements, Dimon's philanthropic efforts have also made a substantial impact. Under his leadership, JPMorgan Chase has invested billions in community development initiatives, education, and job training programs, demonstrating a commitment to supporting local communities and creating opportunities for underserved populations.

As Dimon's career eventually comes to a close, his legacy will be defined not only by the success of JPMorgan Chase but also by the values and principles he has championed throughout his tenure. He has shown that leadership is about more than just achieving financial success; it's about making a positive impact, inspiring others, and leaving the world a better place than you found it.

His career offers a blueprint for effective leadership in the modern business world. His emphasis on integrity, resilience, and innovation has left a lasting mark on the financial industry and serves as a source of inspiration for the next generation of business leaders. As we reflect on his legacy, it's clear that his influence will be felt for many years to come, both within JPMorgan Chase and across the broader business landscape.

Made in the USA
Columbia, SC
16 February 2025

53956166R00039